Half Yard
Home

Half Yard

Home

Easy sewing projects using
left-over pieces of fabric

Debbie Shore

SEARCH PRESS

First published in Great Britain 2014

Search Press Limited
Wellwood, North Farm Road,
Tunbridge Wells, Kent TN2 3DR

Photographs by Garie Hind
Styling by Kimberley Hind

ISBN: 978-1-78221-108-2

Suppliers
For details of suppliers, please visit the
Search Press website: www.searchpress.com.

Printed in China

Acknowledgements

My family are heavily involved in
my books: my husband Garie is the
photographer, my daughter Kimberley is
my stylist and model, and my son Tyler,
niece Lorna and her daughter Hettie
have all modelled for me in this book,
so thank you all for helping without
question when I needed you!

I've been sewing now for over fifty years. My mum was a dressmaker, so I was brought up to 'make do and mend' like many people of my generation. Although most of my career has been in front of the camera, my favourite place is behind the sewing machine! I'm very lucky now that my TV work involves sewing, so my two passions are combined! I get the most satisfaction from inspiring new sewers, and the popularity of my books, which are filled with simple projects that suit a beginner.
If you gain pleasure from your new hobby and can save a bit of money as well, you've made me a very happy lady!

Contents

Yo-yo Cloth,
page 18

Cube Basket,
page 20

Magazine Box,
page 22

Napkins,
page 38

Napkin Rings,
page 40

Table Runner,
page 42

Bag Dispenser,
page 58

Coffee Cosy,
page 60

Tablet Holder,
page 62

Bunting,
page 80

Garment Protector,
page 82

Vase Sleeve,
page 24

Reversible Knitting Bag,
page 26

Coasters,
page 32

Place Mats,
page 34

Hanging Heart,
page 36

Picture Frame,
page 44

Fabric Bowl,
page 46

Chair Slip,
page 48

Apron,
page 52

Oven Mitt,
page 54

Tea Cosy,
page 64

Café Curtain,
page 68

Lavender Heart,
page 70

Pumpkin Pillow,
page 72

Jewellery Roll,
page 76

Picnic Place Mat
page 86

Bread Bag,
page 88

Jar Cover,
page 90

Picnic Pillow,
page 92

Bottle Bag,
page 94

Introduction

I have enjoyed making the projects in this book so much! It's so satisfying to take a small piece of fabric to create something that improves the look or the comfort of the place you live in. I take so much pleasure in matching the colours and patterns of fabric and embellishing with buttons, beads and bows. Gifts that are hand sewn are always received so excitedly and ultimately you'll save money by making them! And don't worry if you're not stitch-perfect, it's nice to see that your items are genuinely handmade.

I decide on the look of the room, then the colour that suits, so I chose a modern look with green and black for the kitchen; romance for the bedroom, which just had to involve floral fabrics; and I wanted to add texture to my shabby chic dining room with lots of lace and bows, so kept the colour to a pastel palette. The picnic table is rustic, so I chose earthy tones, and my plain living room was just asking for a splash of colour!

The beauty of decorating a room with smaller items is that if you change your mind and want a different feel, it doesn't cost the earth to make the projects again in different colours.

Each project will take up to half a yard of fabric, though for items like the place mats and cushion covers, you may wish to buy more fabric if you want to make more than one. I try not to use patterns, as I find it easier to use household items to make templates – I have a pantry full of things to draw round! My seam allowance is ¼in (0.5cm) for most projects, unless I have stated otherwise in the instructions.

For me, homeware is certainly where the heart is!

Useful things

Fabric: I use 100% woven cotton fabric and never throw away even the smallest scrap; it will always come in useful! Calico is a natural cotton fabric that is low cost and good to use when it will not be seen, as in the Tablet Holder project on page 62.

Thread: always use a quality thread, as this way your seams will be stronger. I keep a large range of colours in a plastic tub so I always have the right match for my fabric.

Sewing machine: you don't need anything special for the projects in this book; a machine that delivers a straight stitch and a zigzag stitch will be fine.

Scissors: a good quality pair of dressmaking shears will be well worth the investment, and you'll find a pair of small scissors useful as well, for snipping threads.

Air erasable pen: I use these frequently to draw around templates. The ink disappears after a few hours.

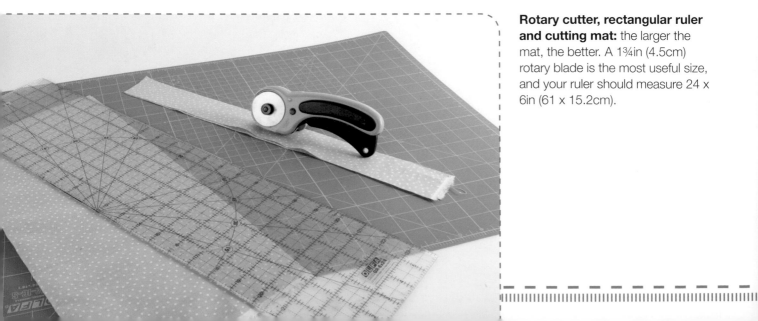

Rotary cutter, rectangular ruler and cutting mat: the larger the mat, the better. A 1¾in (4.5cm) rotary blade is the most useful size, and your ruler should measure 24 x 6in (61 x 15.2cm).

Hand sewing needles: I mostly use sharps, but keep a range of different sizes in your sewing box, for various thicknesses of thread.

Pins: I like to use glass-headed pins for a couple of reasons: I can see them if I drop any, and if I catch them with the iron, the heads don't melt!

Seam ripper: your sewing machine will probably come with a seam ripper or 'quick unpick', but they do blunt with use so always have a spare. Use these for undoing the occasional mistake – they do happen!

Plastic tape measure: plastic does not distort like fabric or wood, so is more accurate.

Tweezers: for plucking away the little threads left after unpicking stitches.

Loop turner: this long hook is the perfect tool to turn out tubes of fabric, and I also used it to pull through the button thread on my Pumpkin Pillow (page 72).

Adhesives: repositionable adhesive spray is very useful for keeping layers of fabric together before sewing. Strong fabric glue will adhere embellishments on projects that don't need to be washed. Silicone glue is used to help fabric from slipping on another surface, as in the Vase Sleeve on page 24. A hot glue gun can be used to attach embellishments.

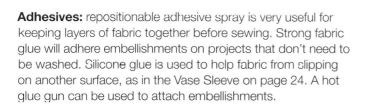

Before you start

Here are some useful tips, stitches and sewing terms before you start sewing:

- Take your time measuring and cutting fabric. If your stitching is wrong, you can always unpick, but if you cut your fabric wrongly, it could cost you more fabric.
- If you're not too good at sewing in a straight line, put a piece of tape over the flat bed of your sewing machine to use as a guide.
- Change your machine needle after approximately eight hours of sewing; a blunt needle can pucker your fabric.
- Good lighting is essential for successful sewing. Daylight bulbs allow you to see the true colours.
- Always use good quality thread. There's a time and place for saving money, but don't skimp when it comes to thread! Cheap thread can break easily and shed fibres into your sewing machine.
- Many fabrics nowadays are pre-shrunk, but if you're not sure, wash and dry your fabric before cutting it.
- Ironing is an important part of sewing. Your seams will sit better and you'll have a more professional finish if you iron them as you go. Pre-ironed fabric is easier to work with.
- Always use sharp scissors, and never use your fabric scissors to cut paper, as it will blunt them.

A piece of tape stuck down on the flat bed of your machine, as shown, will help you sew in a straight line.

Machine stitch

STRAIGHT STITCH

This is used to sew fabric together. Use an 8–6 stitches per inch (3–4mm) length for seams and a longer stitch for top stitching.

Hand sewing stitches

Familiarise yourself with the following stitches and, though really simple to learn, they will give your sewing project a neat, professional finish.

TACKING/BASTING

This is a rough running stitch used to hold fabric together temporarily, for example for a zip insertion. Don't worry if the stitches are not even or the thread is the wrong colour, as these stitches will be pulled out after machine stitching.

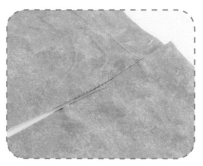

LADDER STITCH

Used to close an opening, as in the lining of the Reversible Knitting Bag (page 26). Make the stitches as small and even as you can, taking the thread evenly from one side of the opening to the other, then gently drawing up to close the opening.

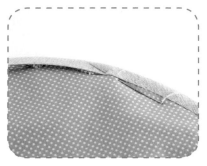

SLIP STITCH

I use this stitch to attach bias binding, as in the Place Mats (page 34). The needle goes through the fabric, then catches a small thread of the bias binding.

OVER EDGE STITCH

This stitch can usually be seen, so keep it as neat as you can. It is used to attach the Bunting pennants to the cord (page 81). The needle comes through the fabric each time from the back, taking the thread over the edge as you sew.

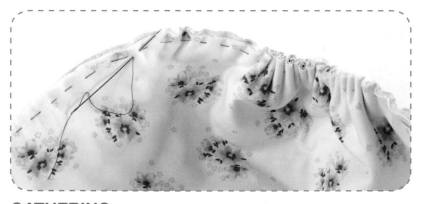

GATHERING

Knot the end of your thread, then stitch a tacking stitch about ¼in (0.5cm) long, close to the edge. When pulled, the fabric gathers up. This is used in the Fabric Bowl (page 46).

Sewing terms

SEAM ALLOWANCE

This is the distance between your stitches and the edge of the fabric. I tend to use a ¼in (0.5cm) seam allowance for the projects in this book, unless otherwise stated.

RAW EDGE

The edge of the fabric that has not been hemmed. If you have a fabric that frays easily, you may wish to sew a zigzag stitch along the raw edge to help stop this. Some machines have a 'mock overlock' stitch that is designed for just this.

BACK TACK

At the start and end of your stitch line, reverse a couple of stitches to stop the stitches from coming undone. Some sewing machines have a 'locking stitch' which places a few stitches on top of each other to secure them.

TOP STITCH

A stitch that is seen on the top of your fabric, used as either a decorative finish or to help keep seams flat. Used on the pocket of the Picnic Place Mat (page 86).

SNIP ACROSS THE CORNERS

Do this on projects like the Picnic Pillow (page 92); this helps to reduce bulk in the corners.

WADDING/BATTING

For most of my projects I use a ¹⁄₈in (3mm) natural wadding/batting, as I find it easier to work with than polyester and it has a quality feel to it. For items like the Place Mats (page 34), I use a heat-resistant type, which is still quite fine but has a silvery reflective quality to help protect your surfaces from heat.

SNIP INTO THE CURVE

Cut a little 'v' shape into the curve of the seam to help reduce the bulk of fabric when turned, allowing the seam to sit flatter. This is used for the Reversible Knitting Bag (page 26), for example. Sometimes you may be able to do this with pinking shears, since these snip little 'v' shapes automatically.

BIAS BINDING

This is a strip of fabric cut along a 45 degree angle to the warp and weft, to give it stretch when going around curves. Bias binding is folded lengthwise, with the edges meeting in the middle, and is machine stitched to the right side of your fabric, along the crease line.

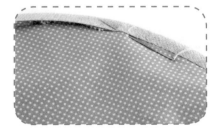

1 Fold over the starting end by ¼in (0.5cm) to neaten before stitching round the edge.

2 When the two ends of the tape come together, overlap the end by about ½in (13mm).

3 Take the bias binding tape over the raw edge, and slip stitch by hand (see page 13) to secure. You can also machine stitch, but the stitches will show through to the right side.

Calculating a circle's circumference

This is needed for the Bread Bag (page 88) from the Picnic chapter. If the circle for the base of the bag measures 8in (20.3cm) in diameter, multiply this by 3.14 to achieve the measurement of the circumference. When cutting the fabric, allow a little extra for the seam allowance.

THE LIVING ROOM

This is a room for relaxation, entertaining, reading or listening to music, so I've kept the colour scheme soft and calm. I had a lot of fun making the yo-yos, and as a theme for a room, I thought they were a little different! The Reversible Knitting Bag could easily be a handbag, the Cube Basket would be just as useful in the kitchen, and the little Yo-yo Cloth could be made much larger for the dining room. Sizes and fabrics can be changed to suit any room, so I hope you will take inspiration from the designs and adapt them for your own home.

Yo-yo Cloth

I have themed my sitting area with these cute yo-yos. They can be made in any size from scraps of fabric, and I find it quite relaxing hand sewing them together. I have then edged a fat quarter with them to make a pretty little cloth for a living room table or bedside cabinet. It would also make a great tray cloth.

What you need:

Circles of fabric, mine measure 5in (12.7cm) across

Needle and thread

Buttons

A fat quarter of cotton fabric

1 Thread a needle, knot your thread and sew a running stitch all around the circumference of the circle, about ¼in (0.5cm) from the edge.

2 Pull up to gather. As I will be covering the stitches with a button, it does not matter if you still see the raw edges. I find this easier than trying to tuck in the edges to make them neat.

3 Don't cut the thread yet, but sew over the gathering a couple of times.

4 Sew on your button. You could sew straight through the button to attach to your project.

5 I found I could make 36 yo-yos from half a yard of fabric, enough to trim a fat quarter, with a few left over. Sew together a string of yo-yos by hand and keep measuring the string against your fabric until it is long enough.

6 Hem the edge of the fat quarter by turning over twice and top stitching.

7 Attach your string of yo-yos by sewing through the buttons and into the fat quarter of fabric.

Tip
Try making up the yo-yos in different sizes and mixing them together.

Cube Basket

This soft fabric cube makes a pretty place to put things to keep you organised. It would also make a charming fruit or bread basket.

What you need:

10 squares of fabric measuring 9in (23cm)

Yo-yo to decorate, see page 18

Needle and thread

1 Sew four squares together in a row, right sides together.

2 Join together to make a tube.

3 Take another square and pin, then sew into the base of the tube. You'll see the cube shape starting to form.

4 Repeat with the remaining five squares to make a lining cube, but leave a gap of around 3in (7.6cm) at one side of the bottom seam for turning.

5 Still inside out, sew together the two cubes all the way around the top.

6 Turn the right way out, then push the lining inside the cube. Sew the opening closed by hand, using a ladder stitch (see page 13).

7 Press, then fold over the top of the cube. Hand-sew the yo-yo onto the cube to decorate.

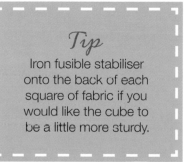

Tip

Iron fusible stabiliser onto the back of each square of fabric if you would like the cube to be a little more sturdy.

Magazine Box

Who would know that underneath this pretty fabric there is a cardboard box! Keep your magazines and books tidy, or use this in your home office to store files and paperwork. I used two fat quarters of fabric for the project.

What you need:

Two rectangles of strong card measuring 13 x 7in (33 x 17.8cm)

Two pieces of strong card measuring 7 x 4in (17.8 x 10cm)

One piece of strong card for the base, measuring 13 x 4in (33 x 10cm)

For the outside of the box: two pieces of fabric measuring 14 x 8in (35.5 x 20.3cm); two pieces measuring 8 x 5in (20.3 x 12.7cm) and one piece measuring 14 x 5in (35.5 x 12.7cm)

For the lining, two pieces of contrasting fabric measuring 14 x 12in (35.5 x 30.5cm); two pieces measuring 5 x 12in (12.7 x 30.5cm) and one piece for the base measuring 14 x 5in (35.5 x 12.7cm)

42in (106.5cm) ribbon to decorate

Repositionable adhesive spray

Fabric glue

A yo-yo to decorate (see page 18)

1 Take the outer fabric and sew the four sides together. Pin then sew the base so you now have a fabric box. Turn the right way out.

2 Spray each cardboard panel with repositionable adhesive spray and carefully put into position on the inside of your fabric box, smoothing out any wrinkles. If you're using corrugated cardboard, spray the smooth side, as you would see the ridges through the fabric.

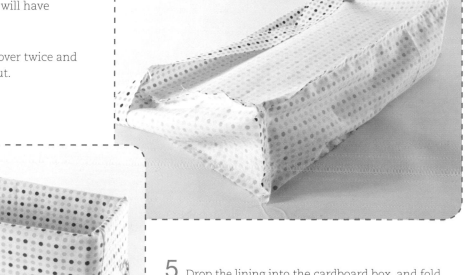

3 Sew together the lining fabric to make another box shape (this one will have longer sides).

4 Hem the top by turning over twice and top stitching. Leave inside out.

5 Drop the lining into the cardboard box, and fold the top over. This should fit quite snugly.

6 Glue the ribbon all the way round to decorate, then add your yo-yo with a spot of fabric glue. Fold a length of ribbon and pop it underneath the yo-yo to make it look like a rosette.

Vase Sleeve

Add a touch of decadence to a plain glass cylinder vase with this pretty sleeve. It makes a bunch of flowers feel like a spectacular bouquet!

What you need:

For a cylinder vase measuring 7in (17.8cm) tall and 9½in (24cm) in circumference:

Outer fabric measuring 6 x 12in (15.2 x 30.5cm)

Lining fabric measuring the same

Fabric for the pleated top measuring 26 x 6in (66 x 15.2cm)

28in (71cm) ribbon to decorate

A yo-yo to decorate (see page 18)

Silicone glue

1 Lay the outer and lining fabrics right sides together and sew with a ¼in (0.5cm) seam allowance around three sides, leaving the top open.

2 Snip across the corners and turn the right way out. Press.

3 Fold the top of the sleeve inwards by about ½in (13mm) and press.

4 For the pleats, fold the long strip of fabric in half lengthways and press, folding each short end inwards by about ½in (13mm). Top stitch the two shorter ends.

5 Begin to pleat by folding and pinning the fabric; you should aim to have a strip the same width as the fabric sleeve. I don't tend to measure – if your pinned pleats are too long or too short, you can alter before sewing. When you have the right length of pleated trim, sew across the bottom to secure.

6 Pin this pleated trim inside the opening of the sleeve.

7 Sew across the top of the sleeve to hold the pleated fabric in place.

8 Attach the ribbon centrally to the back of the vase sleeve with a few machine stitches.

> *Tip*
> This sleeve is easily adapted for a larger vase, but you may need to put a couple of ribbons around it. If the fabric slips on the glass, put a few drops of silicone glue on the inside of the sleeve and leave to dry. This will help the sleeve to grip the vase.

9 Wrap around your vase and tie in a bow. Position your yo-yo where it sits well and pin then sew it in place.

Reversible Knitting Bag

This is a handy bag in which to keep your knitting, and it would make an equally stylish baby bag, beach bag or handbag! Turn it inside out and you have a different look; making this a two-in-one bag for a lady on the go!

What you need:

Two rectangles of fabric in pattern 1 measuring 20 x 10in (51 x 25.5cm)

Two rectangles in pattern 2 measuring 20 x 10in (51 x 25.5cm)

Four pieces of contrast fabric for the top of the bag measuring 13 x 3in (33 x 7.5cm)

For the handles, two strips measuring 20 x 3in (51 x 7.5cm) and a yo-yo to decorate (see page 18)

A saucer to use as a template and a pencil

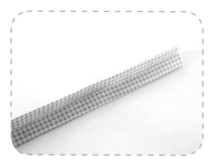

1 For the handles, take each long strip of fabric and press in half lengthways. Press the two long sides inwards, fold in half so you don't see the raw edges, and top stitch down both sides.

2 Take all four bag sections, draw round the saucer on each bottom corner and cut to round off the corners.

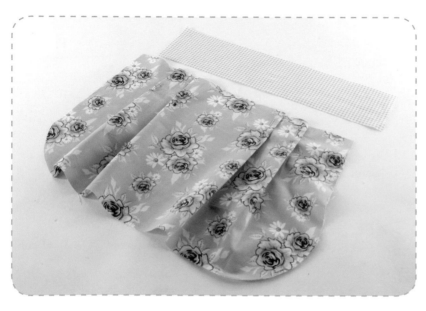

3 Lay a top strip of fabric onto your table. Place the bottom section underneath; it will of course be wider. Pinch four pleats at equal distance from the centre of the bottom section, until it is the same width as the top. Pin.

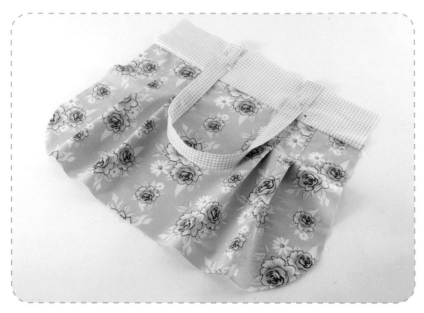

4 Do the same with all four sides, keeping the pleats in the same place on each section. Sew across the top of the pleats to keep them in place when the pins come out, then neatly top stitch about 3in (7.5cm) down each pleat.

5 Pin the handles to the top of each pattern 1 side, in line with the pleats, facing inwards.

6 Sew one side of pattern 1 to one side of pattern 2, right sides together, across the top. Repeat with the second side.

7 Place the two bag sections right sides together, pattern 1 to pattern 1 and pattern 2 to pattern 2.

8 Sew all the way round, leaving a gap of about 3in (7.6cm) at the base for turning. Snip into the curves to make the seams lie flat.

9 Turn the bag the right way out, and sew across the opening with a ladder stitch (see page 13).

10 Push one side of the bag inside the other, and press.

11 Turn inside out for a different look! Decorate with a yo-yo attached with a safety pin so that you can pin it to either side.

Tip
The bag can easily be made larger or smaller, with the handles longer or shorter, so you could make a matching purse!

THE DINING ROOM

I think the dining room is the easiest room to sew for, which is why there are so many projects in this chapter! I have chosen pastel, vintage-inspired fabrics to keep the room bright but soft, and I think they create a pleasant feel that does not detract from whatever is on the menu – in this case cupcakes! The dining room is a place for entertaining, company and conversation, and my shabby chic tones set the scene for a calm but classy tea time.

Coasters

These are simple slip-over coasters for wine glasses that help to protect your table from drips. They can also be made in a different colour for each guest, so they can identify their drinks when leaving the table! Measure across the base of the glass for a perfect fit; my glasses measured 2½in (6.4cm) across.

What you need

For each coaster:

Two matching circles of fabric measuring 3in (7.5cm) across (I used a saucer as a template)

One circle of base fabric measuring the same

One circle of ⅛in (3mm) wadding/batting measuring the same

6in (15.2cm) lace

Paper flower for decoration, or if the coasters are to be washed, use a button

32

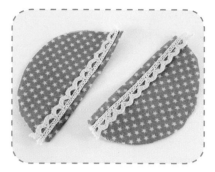

1 Take the two matching circles and fold each in half. Press, then sew a strip of lace along each straight side.

2 Place the base fabric right side up, lay the circle of wadding/batting on top, then on top of that the lace-edged pieces, face down. Pin.

3 Machine stitch all the way around, with a ¼in (0.5cm) seam allowance.

4 Trim back to about ⅛in (3mm) from the seam, then turn the right way out and press.

5 Sew the paper flower or button just off-centre.

Tip
Use a circle of oilcloth for the base of the coaster to stop it from slipping.

Place Mats

Dress your table in style with these vintage-inspired place mats – it seems a shame to cover them up! I printed an image of cutlery onto printable cotton fabric, then used a hot, steam-free iron to set the ink so that the place mat is wipeable.

What you need:

- One 12in (30.5cm) diameter circle each of top fabric, base fabric and heat-resistant wadding/batting
- Strips of ribbon and lace, 7ft (2.13m) in total
- 40in (102cm) of 1in (2.5cm) bias binding
- Printable cotton fabric printed with an image of cutlery from an old book
- Three buttons in coordinating colours

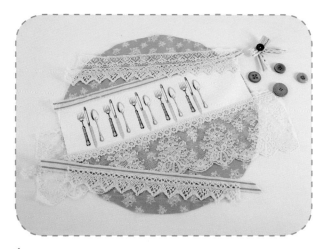

1 Place the base circle face down, lay the wadding/batting on top, then the top fabric right side up on top of that. Pin all the way round, then tack/baste close to the edge to hold in place.

2 Lay the printed sheet of fabric across the circle at an angle. When you're happy, top stitch it in place on your machine.

3 Repeat with the strips of lace and ribbon, adding one at a time and building the look until you're happy with it.

4 Add the buttons and bow by hand, keeping them to the edge of the mat but remembering to allow room for the bias binding.

5 Apply the bias binding all the way around the circle, then hand sew to the back. The fabric may start to curl, but don't worry, it will flatten out when you press it.

6 Press, stretching the bias binding if you need to.

Tip
When making up the remaining place mats, sew the lace and ribbon strips at different angles to give each one a unique look.

Hanging Heart

This pretty decoration adds a touch of romance to the dining room and can be made to any size you like. It's a good way of using up scraps of ribbon and lace, and makes an affordable piece of art!

What you need:

A piece of card measuring 16in (40.5cm) square, a pen and a 7in (17.8cm) diameter plate to make a template

Two pieces of fabric measuring 14in (35.5cm) square, one for the front and one for the lining

Spray starch

About a yard (91cm) of lace

Half a yard (46cm) each of two colours of ribbon

A couple of buttons

Self-adhesive gems

Fabric glue

1 Draw a line down the centre of the card. Place the plate slightly over the line and draw around it.

2 Measure 11in (28cm) down from where this circle meets the top of the line and join this point to the side of the circle.

3 Fold in half along the line and cut to make your heart template. Cut one heart from the top fabric and one from the lining fabric.

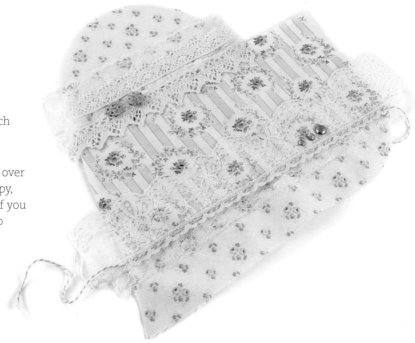

4 Spray both pieces of fabric with starch and leave to dry.

5 Now for the decorating! Lay the lace over the top fabric and trim when you're happy, then sew or glue in place. Gluing is fine if you prefer, as this decoration is unlikely to go in the wash! Add the buttons and any other embellishments you have.

6 Lay the heart pieces right sides together and sew all the way round, leaving a gap at the side of around 3in (7.6cm) for turning. Turn right sides out, press, then sew the opening closed with a ladder stitch (see page 13).

7 Loop 5in (12.7cm) of ribbon and hand sew to the top of the heart to hang, then add a couple of bows to the base of the loop.

Tip
If your fabric is very lightweight, use a fusible stabiliser to help stiffen it.

Napkins

It is the finishing touches that make a difference, and these simple napkins perfectly fit the bill! The lace trim adds a touch of style and is in keeping with my shabby chic theme, but does not detract from the decoration on the napkin rings I have made to go with these napkins (see page 40).

(see page 40).

What you need:

For each napkin:
Two squares of fabric measuring 9in (23cm)
37in (94cm) lace trim

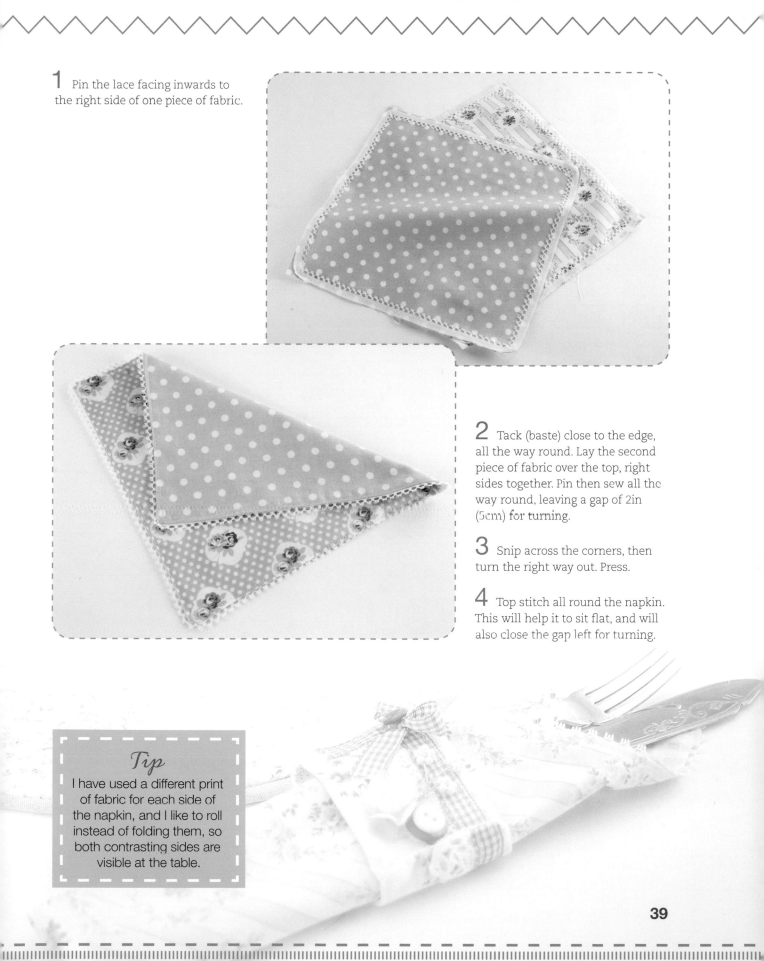

1 Pin the lace facing inwards to the right side of one piece of fabric.

2 Tack (baste) close to the edge, all the way round. Lay the second piece of fabric over the top, right sides together. Pin then sew all the way round, leaving a gap of 2in (5cm) for turning.

3 Snip across the corners, then turn the right way out. Press.

4 Top stitch all round the napkin. This will help it to sit flat, and will also close the gap left for turning.

Tip

I have used a different print of fabric for each side of the napkin, and I like to roll instead of folding them, so both contrasting sides are visible at the table.

Napkin Rings

I had so much fun making these napkin rings. As they are not going in the wash, I used paper flowers and buttons to decorate them. You could experiment with dried flowers, beads or embellishments you have made yourself with clay or card.

What you need:

For each napkin ring:

Two rectangles of fabric measuring 7 x 3in (17.8 x 7.5cm)

Strip of ribbon measuring 7in (17.8cm) long

Strip of lace measuring 7in (17.8cm) long

2in (5cm) of elastic cord

Button to fasten

Three buttons to decorate

Three small paper flowers

Hot glue gun

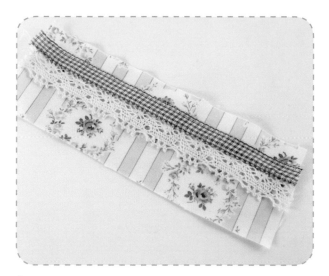

1 Sew the ribbon and lace strips to the right side of the front of the napkin ring fabric.

2 Loop the elastic cord and pin, facing inwards, to one of the short ends of the fabric. Secure with a couple of stitches and remove the pin.

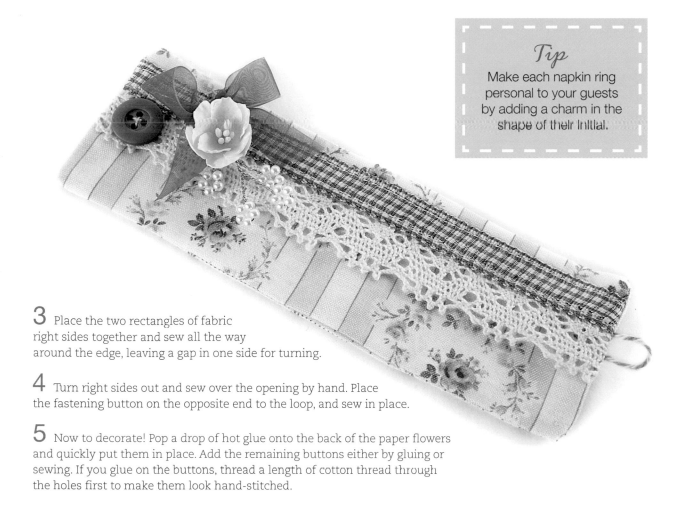

Tip
Make each napkin ring personal to your guests by adding a charm in the shape of their initial.

3 Place the two rectangles of fabric right sides together and sew all the way around the edge, leaving a gap in one side for turning.

4 Turn right sides out and sew over the opening by hand. Place the fastening button on the opposite end to the loop, and sew in place.

5 Now to decorate! Pop a drop of hot glue onto the back of the paper flowers and quickly put them in place. Add the remaining buttons either by gluing or sewing. If you glue on the buttons, thread a length of cotton thread through the holes first to make them look hand-stitched.

Table Runner

Add style and character to your dining with this decorative table runner, which can help to protect your table.

1 Your canvas will be shorter than the runner, so add a piece of the 11 x 7in (28 x 17.7cm) fabric to the top and bottom, to bring it to an 18in (45.7cm) length. Lay this section centrally on top of the calico.

2 Place the first strip of fabric face down and at a slight angle over the central panel, making sure the edges overlap, and sew.

3 Fold back and press. Repeat with the second strip of fabric.

4 Continue until the calico is covered.

5 Sew your ribbon and lace over the seams, or at an angle, across the piece, whichever you think looks better.

6 Trim away the excess fabric to the calico, then place the wadding/batting on top, followed by the lining fabric, face down.

7 Sew all the way around, leaving a gap of about 4in (10cm) for turning. Turn right sides out and press.

8 Sew closed the opening by hand with ladder stitch (see page 13).

9 Top stitch about 1in (2.5cm) from the hem, all the way round the runner. This will help to keep the wadding/batting in place.

10 Finish by hand, sewing your buttons and bows on, but remember to keep them away from the centre of your table runner if you are going to put hot plates there!

Picture Frame

There's no sewing involved here, but I just thought the frame deserved a mention as it matches my shabby chic dining room perfectly! This frame was really inexpensive pale wood that I thought would make a good backdrop for the lace. The photograph is of my Mum and Dad on their wedding day.

What you need:

A picture frame and photograph

Card the same size as the frame

Strips of lace and ribbon, about 1½ yards (1.62m) in total

Fabric-covered buttons

Two hat pins

Hot glue gun

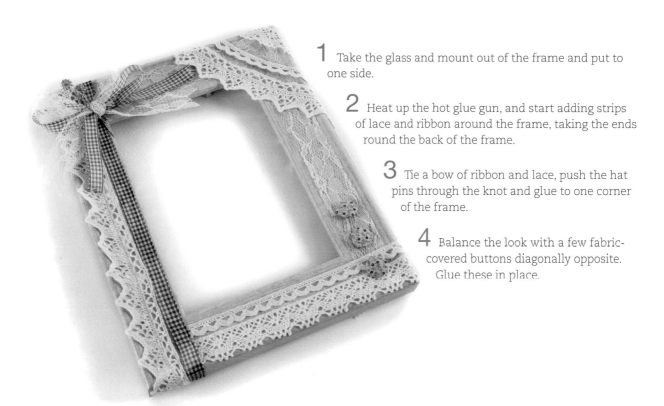

1 Take the glass and mount out of the frame and put to one side.

2 Heat up the hot glue gun, and start adding strips of lace and ribbon around the frame, taking the ends round the back of the frame.

3 Tie a bow of ribbon and lace, push the hat pins through the knot and glue to one corner of the frame.

4 Balance the look with a few fabric-covered buttons diagonally opposite. Glue these in place.

5 Trim the photograph if needed and place back in the frame behind the glass.

6 Cut a piece of card to the size of the frame and glue over the back to hide the ends of the ribbon and lace.

Tip
Paper or dried flowers could be glued to the frame. If you are using a colour photograph, try to match the colours in the picture with the colours of your decorations.

Fabric Bowl

This useful little bowl looks great on the dining table as a bread basket, though here we have gone for cake instead! It would look just as good in the bedroom as a cotton wool ball holder, and makes a perfect place for keeping keys, sewing machine bobbins or jewellery. I used a dinner plate as a template for the circles.

What you need:

Two circles of fabric, outer and lining, 12in (30.5cm) in diameter

One circle of $\frac{1}{8}$in (3mm) wadding/batting the same size

14in (35.5cm) of 1in (2.5cm) wide bias binding

12in (30.5cm) lace

12in (30.5cm) ribbon

Button to decorate

1 Lay the outer fabric patterned side down. Lay the wadding/batting on top, then the lining fabric on top of that, patterned side up.

2 Hand sew a tacking/basting stitch all the way round the circumference, quite close to the edge.

3 Gently pull the thread to gather the fabric. Keep the gathers even, then secure the end of the thread by oversewing a few stitches.

4 Sew the bias binding to the outside of the top bowl with your sewing machine.

5 Fold over the bias binding and hand sew the inside. Knot the ribbon and lace together in a bow, and attach to the join in the bias binding by sewing through the button.

Tip
Make the bowl up in different sizes by using smaller or larger templates. A matching set of three would look lovely!

Chair Slip

Dress your dining chairs to impress with these pretty padded slip covers, coordinating with your table mats and accessories to create a delightful eating area for your family and guests. The use of wadding/batting makes the slip comfortable to sit back on, and helps it keep its shape.

What you need

For each slip:

Half a yard (46cm) of cotton fabric, cut into two halves; I used a quarter yard (23cm) each of two patterns

Half a yard (46cm) each of lining fabric and fusible wadding/batting

40in (101.6cm) ribbon

36in (91.4cm) lace trim

Card and a pen to make a template

1 Place your card on the floor and lay the chair on its back on top. Draw around the outline of the top of the chair back, and measure 18in (46cm) down. Cut out the shape 1in (2.5cm) larger than the pen line, and if your chair has any detail on the frame, cut round this in a curve.

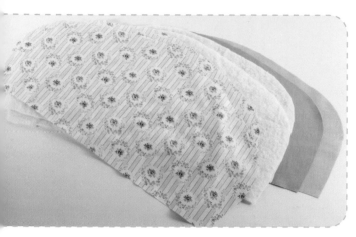

2 Fold in half widthways to check the template is symmetrical. Place on top of the two pieces of fabric, draw round the outline and cut out. Cut two pieces the same from the lining fabric.

3 Iron the fusible wadding/batting to the wrong sides of the fabric and trim.

4 Right sides together, sew the straight edge of the lining to the straight edge of the padded fabric.

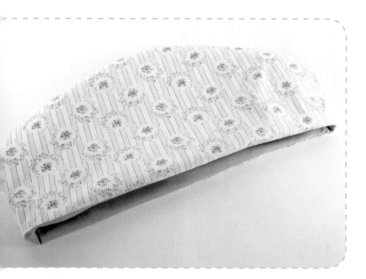

5 Open up the two sides, and pin right sides together. Sew all the way round with a ¼in (0.5cm) seam allowance, leaving a gap at the top of the lining for turning.

6 Turn the right way out, and hand sew the opening to close with a ladder stitch (see page 13). Push the lining inside the slip and press.

7 Pin the lace and ribbon round the bottom of the slip, and using the free arm on your sewing machine if you have one, sew in place. Add a bow to one side and top with a button.

Tip
If you are using a trim with beads, attach it on the back of the chair slip only, as it will be uncomfortable to lean back on.

THE KITCHEN

Offset against black doors and pale worktops, the lime greens and blues in these kitchen projects really pop! In this chapter we will be making a coordinating Bag Dispenser for plastic bags, an Apron, Cafetière Cosy, Tablet Holder, Tea Cosy and matching Oven Mitt. I have used 100% cotton fabric and where wadding/batting is needed, a thickness of $\frac{1}{8}$in (3mm) is fine.

A walking foot is useful for helping to feed several layers of fabric through the sewing machine without slippage. And don't stop just with these projects; the Café Curtain (page 68) from the Bedroom section may fit your kitchen window and some of the projects from the Living Room secion might also come in handy in the kitchen. Use your imagination and fill the kitchen with colour!

Apron

Turn housework into a style statement with this little apron that is almost too cute to get messy! I have used a woven cotton fabric that is washable, lined it to add weight and added a useful pocket to the front. I decided the white tape I used for the tie was too stark, so I sewed coloured bias binding of the same length over the top.

What you need:

Rectangle of patterned fabric measuring 16 X 22in (40.5 x 56cm)

Rectangle of lining fabric the same size; I used the same fabric because I had so much of it

Contrast fabric for the pocket measuring 9 x 15in (23 x 38cm)

Lining fabric for the pocket measuring the same

Tape for the ties measuring 8ft (2.44m), plus bias binding the same length

72½in (104cm) bias binding

An 8in (20.3cm) plate as a template, and an air erasable pen

1 To make the pocket, lay the patterned fabric face down over the lining, and sew round three sides, leaving the top open.

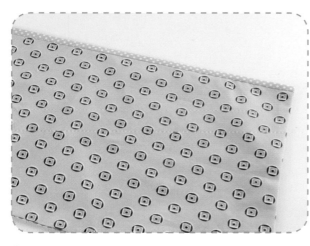

2 Turn the right way out and press. Attach bias binding across the top of the pocket.

3 Take the two rectangles of fabric that make up the apron and lay them right sides together. Use the plate as a template and draw round it at the two bottom corners with the air erasable pen, then cut.

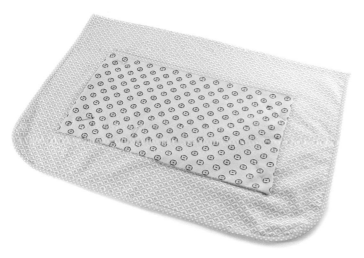

4 Sew the top of the patterned fabric to the top of the lining, right sides together, fold back and press.

5 Pin the two hems together, tack/baste if you like, then sew the bias binding round the raw edge.

6 Place the pocket centrally over the right side of the patterned side, pin in place then sew round the bottom three sides, making sure you back tack at the start and finish (see page 14) to secure the stitches.

7 Pin the bias binding along the tape for the ties and top stitch down both long sides. Fold the tape in half to mark the centre, then place this over the centre of the top of the apron, and top stitch to secure.

Tip
You could decorate the pocket with buttons, or make the tape twice as long and wide so that you can tie it in a big bow at the front!

Oven Mitt

The two-tone colours of this quilted mitt will coordinate with your kitchen perfectly, and will fit any size of hand, left or right! I have used heat-resistant wadding/batting to help protect your hands from the heat.

What you need:

Top fabric, two rectangles measuring 9 x 10in (23 x 25.4cm)

Bottom fabric, two rectangles measuring 8 x 4in (20.3 x 10cm)

Two rectangles of lining fabric measuring 14 x 9in (35.5 x 23in)

¼in (0.5cm) heat-resistant wadding/batting measuring 14 x 9in (35.5 x 23in)

4in (10cm) matching ribbon for the hanging loop

Button

Piece of card and pen to make a template

Air erasable pen and ruler

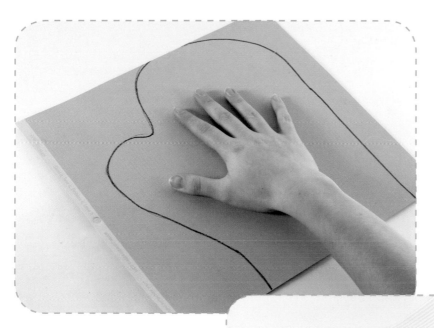

1 Place your hand and wrist on the card and draw a smooth outline about 2½in (6.5cm) around the edge.

2 Cut out the template. Sew the two top pieces of fabric to the bottom pieces, right sides together. Press.

3 Lay these two right sides together with the seams matching up and pin.

4 Place the template over the fabric and draw all the way round, then cut out the mitt shape. Do the same with the wadding/batting and lining fabric.

5 Take both sides of the outer fabric and draw a 2in (5cm) grid with the air erasable pen, on the diagonal.

6 Place the outer fabric wrong side down on top of the wadding/batting and pin. With your walking foot on your sewing machine, sew a straight stitch over the lines to quilt. This looks attractive and helps to keep the wadding/batting in place.

7 Lay each front piece face down on its lining, and sew across the top.

8 Fold the ribbon in half and pin, facing inwards, to the side of the mitt.

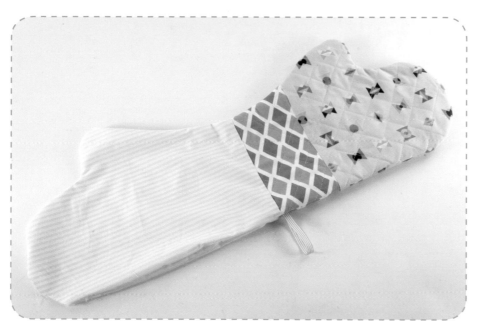

9 Place the two sides face together and pin. Sew all the way around the outside, leaving a gap at the top of the lining of around 3in (7.5cm) for turning. Snip into the curves, turn and close the opening with a ladder stitch (see page 13).

Tip
Instead of a grid, you could free motion stipple all over the mitt. Why not make a pair?

Bag Dispenser

Keep those ugly plastic carrier bags hidden away in a pretty pouch that can hang behind the kitchen door. Pop them in the top and pull them out from the bottom when you need them.

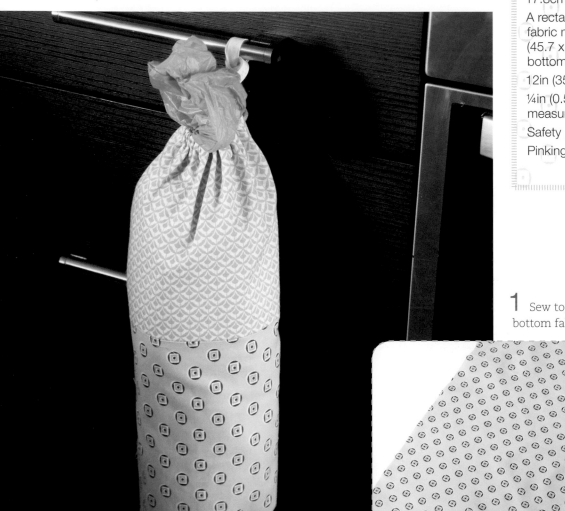

1 Sew together the top and bottom fabrics and press.

2 Cut along the side seams with pinking shears to help stop fraying.

3 Fold the fabric in half right sides together with the pinked edges together, and sew to make a tube, but leave a 2in (5cm) gap at the top end of and a 1in (2.5cm) gap at the bottom.

4 Fold the top over twice, making a wide hem of about 1in (2.5cm). Do the same at the bottom, making a ½in (13mm) hem. Turn the tube the right side out.

5 Push the safety pin through the end of the elastic and use it to thread the elastic through the bottom of the tube, then hand sew the two ends together and tuck them into the seam. Do the same with the cord at the top of the bag, and tie the ends together.

Tip
You could also use the dispenser for storing dusters.

Coffee Cosy

This stylish cafetière cosy will not only keep your coffee hot for longer; it also embraces the bright, zingy feel of our kitchen theme.

Firstly measure your coffee pot to make sure you get a snug fit. Mine measures 12½in (31.7cm) around the pot and the glass is 4½in (11.5cm) tall. So my fabric is cut slightly larger to accommodate the seam allowance, making it 13 x 5in (33 x 12.7cm).

What you need:

Outer fabric measuring 13 x 5in (33 x 12.7cm)

Lining fabric and ⅛in (3mm) cotton wadding/batting measuring the same

For the scallops, a strip of contrasting fabric measuring 13 x 2½in (33 x 6.3cm)

Stabiliser or lightweight cotton fabric measuring the same

Two buttons

Two pieces of ¼in (0.5cm) elastic measuring 4in (10cm) each for the loops

Air erasable pen and circle template measuring 2in (5cm) in diameter (you can draw round a glass on card)

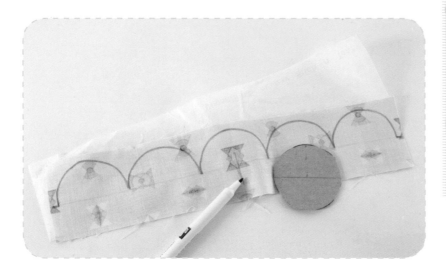

1 To make the scalloped top, mark the centre point of a short side on the reverse of the fabric and draw a line 1½in (3.8cm) from the edge.

2 Cut out your card template and draw a line across the centre. Line the centre of the template up to the line on the fabric and draw round the arc. Repeat all the way across the fabric.

3 Cut round the pen line. Place right side down onto the stabiliser, and sew round the scallops. Cut away the excess stabiliser. Turn the right way out. Press.

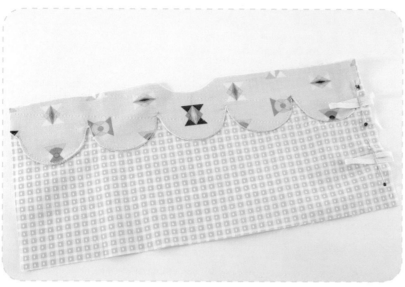

4 Lay this across the top of the main fabric, pin, then top stitch around the scallops.

5 Wrap the fabric around the pot and mark the top and bottom of the inside of the handle with air erasable pen. These will be the positions for the fastening loops. Also mark where the spout will be, as you will need to cut a little curve into the fabric to allow for this.

6 Place the elastic loops on your outer fabric where you made the marks, facing inwards, and pin.

7 On top of this, lay the lining, right side down, then the wadding/batting. Sew all the way round, leaving a gap on one side of about 3in (7.6cm) for turning. The walking foot on your sewing machine will help to stop the layers from slipping as you sew.

8 Snip across the corners and turn the right way out. Hand sew the opening with ladder stitch (see page 13).

9 Fold over the cosy and draw a dot through the loops to mark the position of the buttons. Sew on the buttons and put the kettle on, it's coffee time!

Tip
Use the same technique to make coffee cup covers to match!

Tablet Holder

This lightweight pillow stand will support your tablet in style, horizontally or vertically. Mine is a 7in (17.7cm) tablet, but increase the measurements if you need it to be larger. Great for when you want to follow a recipe or online tutorial in the kitchen!

What you need:

Rectangle of fabric measuring 18 x 11in (45.7 x 27.9cm

A large handful of toy stuffing

½in (13mm) dowelling

Secateurs

Calico pouch measuring 6 x 3in (15.2 x 7.5cm), filled with rice

Two buttons, one a little smaller than the other

Air erasable pen

1 Fold the shorter sides of the rectangle together, right sides facing. Sew across one end and down the side.

2 Turn right sides out. Pinch the two sides of the sewn end and pull them open to form a square. The seam should be at the bottom.

3 Take the point of the square and fold it over to the centre. Pin in place.

4 Sew the buttons, one on top of the other, over this point, but make sure you only attach them to the top layer of fabric so the pillow still opens up.

5 Start to fill with toy stuffing, pushing the pouch of rice into the base of the pillow.

6 Measure 2½in (6.3cm) from the opening, pin the opening as shown and mark a line with air erasable pen. Machine stitch across this line. This may be easier with your zipper foot.

7 Fold the end of the opening in by ¼in (0.5cm) and press, then top stitch across the opening.

8 Cut the dowelling to about 1in (2.5cm) shorter that this length. Dowelling is quite soft and I cut mine to size with the garden secateurs!

9 Place the dowelling under the flap and fold under. Hand sew the fabric into a tube with slip stitch (see page 13), then close each end of the tube with ladder stitch (see page 13).

Tea Cosy

Keep your cuppa warmer for longer with this insulated tea cosy, perfectly matched to coordinate with your stylish kitchen décor!

What you need:

Measure your teapot; mine is 6in (15.3cm) tall and 10in (25.5cm) across from spout to handle, so I have allowed two pieces of fabric for the top section measuring 14 x 7in (35.5 x 17.8cm)

Two pieces for the border measuring 14 x 4in (35.5 x 10cm)

Two pieces of lining fabric measuring 14 x 11½in (35.5 x 29.2cm)

Two pieces of ⅛in (3mm) wadding/batting measuring 14 x 11½in (35.5 x 29.2cm)

3in (7.7cm) length of ¼in (0.5cm) wide ribbon for the hanging loop

A large dinner plate to use as a template, and a pencil

Repositionable adhesive spray

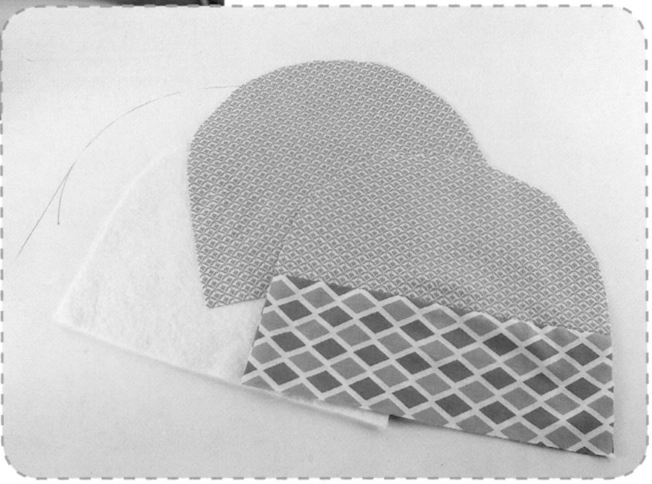

1 Take the top sections of the outer fabric, wadding/batting and lining and, using your dinner plate, draw an arc, then cut to make the domed shape of the cosy.

2 Stitch the top fabric pieces to the border with a ¼in (0.5cm) seam allowance, right sides together. Press.

3 Use repositionable adhesive spray to stick the wadding/batting to the wrong side of the lining.

4 Sew the bottom of the lining to the bottom of the outer fabric.

5 Pin the ribbon loop, facing inwards, to the top of the cosy.

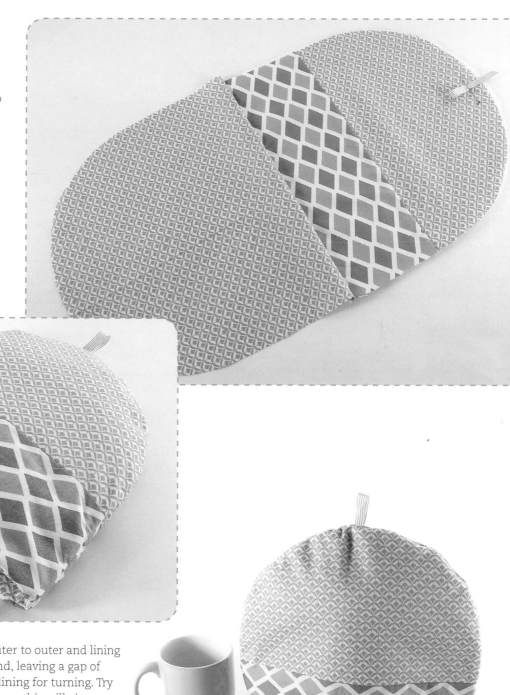

6 Place the two sides together, outer to outer and lining to lining, and sew all the way around, leaving a gap of about 3in (7.5cm) at the top of the lining for turning. Try to make sure your seams match up, as this will give a professional finish.

7 Turn the tea cosy the right way out, and sew across the opening by hand with a ladder stitch (see page 13). Push the lining inside the outer fabric and press.

THE BEDROOM

The bedroom is not just a place to sleep, but also a quiet retreat, a salon, reading space and dressing room. Make yours a pretty place to be with these useful accessories. There is a Jewellery Roll to keep your treasures safe, a Café Curtain to decorate your window, a cute Pumpkin Pillow for the bed, a Garment Protector to keep your favourite dress dust-free, pretty Bunting and a delightful fragranced Lavender Heart, all in relaxing pastel tones.

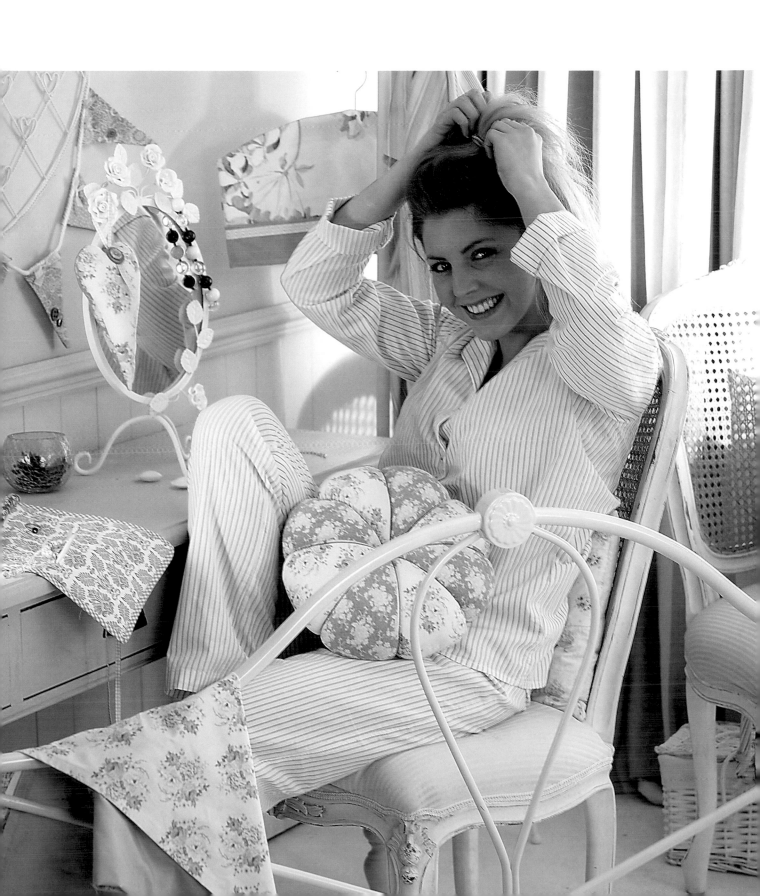

Café Curtain

My curtain took just the half yard of fabric, but I cheated a little as the lining was another half yard. This type of curtain affords privacy while letting in the light, and makes the window a pretty feature of the bedroom. You will need a curtain pole to hang the curtain; I have used an extending one that adjusts to fit into the recess of the window. This way you I don't need to drill into the wall and it won't leave any marks if you change your mind!

What you need:

Main fabric measuring 18 x 36in (45.7 x 91.5cm)

Lining fabric measuring the same

Nine pieces of main fabric measuring 3 x 8in (7.5 x 20.3cm)

Nine lining pieces measuring the same

Nine buttons

Loop turner

1 To make the tab tops, lay the nine fabric rectangles right sides together with the nine lining pieces and sew around three sides, leaving one end open for turning.

2 You may find a loop turner makes the job easier; this is a metal stick with a hook on the end (see page 11). Feed it into the tube and grab the end of the fabric, then simply pull through.

3 Fold over the bottom of the curtain fabric twice by ¼in (0.5cm) and sew to make a hem, then do the same with the lining fabric.

4 Evenly space the nine tabs across the right side of the curtain fabric, raw edges together and facing inwards, and pin.

5 Lay the lining on top of this and pin across the top and sides, then sew all the way round. Turn the right way out and press.

6 Fold over the tabs and secure each one with a button. Thread the curtain pole through and hang the curtain.

Lavender Heart

Add a touch of delicate fragrance to the bedroom with this romantic, lavender-filled hanging heart. If you prefer, use a little essential oil instead of dried lavender.

What you need:

Two pieces of fabric measuring 6 x 10in (15.2 x 25.4cm)

Toy stuffing to fill

A piece of card, pen, ruler and a 2½in (6.3cm) jar lid or similar for the template

Two spoonfuls of dried lavender

Seam ripper

12in (30.5cm) ribbon to hang

Two buttons, different sizes

1 Draw a line down the centre of your card. Place the lid to one side of the line, near the top, slightly overlapping. Draw around it. Repeat on the opposite side of the line.

2 Measure 9in (23cm) down the line and mark, then draw a line with your ruler from the side of each circle to this point. Now you have a heart!

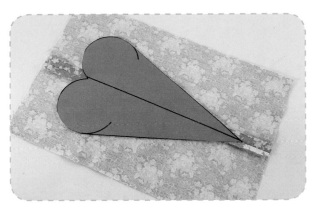

3 Take one of the pieces of fabric to make the back, and cut in half lengthways. Re-sew these two pieces together with a ¼in (0.5) seam allowance. Press the seam open.

4 Place the template centrally over the seam, trace the outline and cut round it.

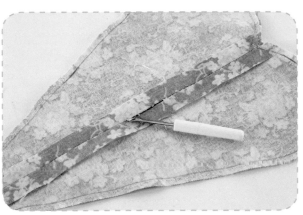

5 Cut the heart shape from the front fabric using the template.

6 With right sides together, pin then sew all the way round the heart. Snip into the curves. Using the seam ripper, undo about 2in (5cm) of stitches from the back seam.

7 Turn the heart the right way out. Stuff with the toy stuffing, adding the dried lavender as you go. Close the opening with a ladder stitch (see page 13).

8 Hand sew the ribbon to the top of the heart and cover your stitches with the buttons.

Tip
If you prefer a fuller shape of heart, make your template with a 5in (12.7cm) depth in the centre instead of 9in (22.8cm).

Pumpkin Pillow

The texture and dimension of this pumpkin pillow give it centre stage in my blue-themed bedroom! Use it among other pillows to dress the bed or, with a little less stuffing, it would make for a very comfortable seat pad.

What you need:

Round pillow pad with a diameter of 12in (30.5cm)

One piece of fabric measuring 13in (33cm) square

A contrasting fabric measuring the same

A loop turner and strong thread

Embroidery needle and thread

Two buttons, one large and one small

A 12in (30.5cm) dinner plate as a template

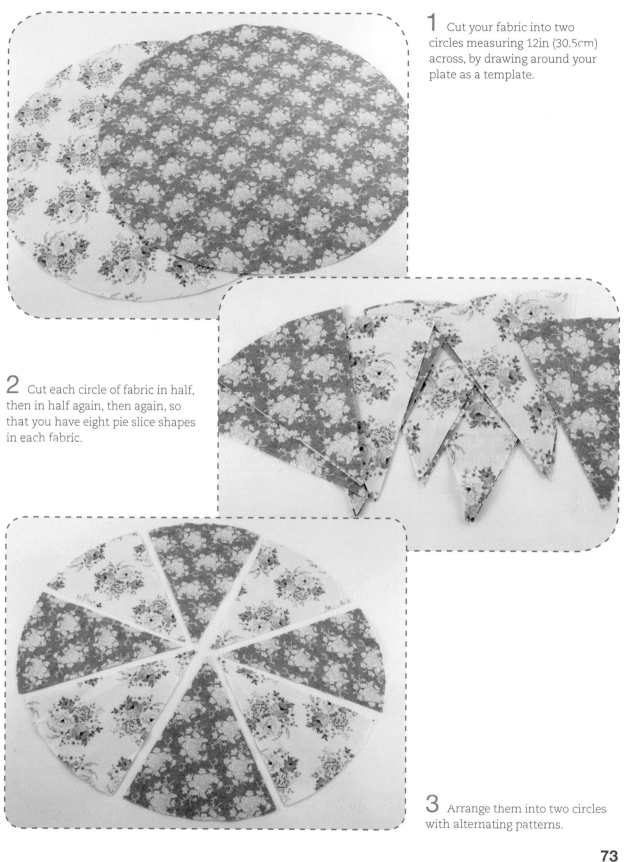

1 Cut your fabric into two circles measuring 12in (30.5cm) across, by drawing around your plate as a template.

2 Cut each circle of fabric in half, then in half again, then again, so that you have eight pie slice shapes in each fabric.

3 Arrange them into two circles with alternating patterns.

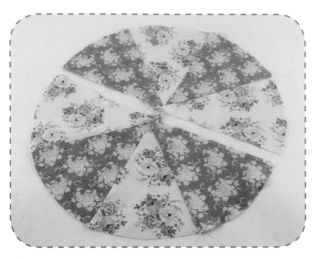

4 Sew four pieces together to make a semicircle, then the next four. Press the seams as you go.

5 Sew the two semicircles together to make a circle and repeat with the other side of the pillow.

6 Lay the two circles right sides together and sew round, carefully matching the seams. Leave a gap of about 6in (15.2cm) for turning. Turn the right way out.

7 Stuff the pillow pad into the cover and sew the opening closed with a ladder stitch (see page 13).

8 Take a piece of embroidery thread, around a yard (92cm) in length. Push the loop turner straight through the centre of the cushion and out the other side, again through the centre point.

9 Grab the embroidery thread and pull through, leaving 1ft (30.5cm) of thread loose.

10 Take the thread over one of the seams to the bottom of the pillow and again push the loop turner through the centre to pull through.

11 Repeat for each seam, pulling the thread tight enough to create the pumpkin look. Pull the thread through carefully as it may tangle due to its length. If you do not have a piece long enough to complete the binding in one go, join another length by knotting at the centre.

12 When you have looped the thread over all eight seams, tie in a knot with the start of the thread.

13 Change to your embroidery needle and, using this thread, attach the two buttons. Knot underneath the buttons and trim away any loose thread.

Tip
I have used only two fabrics, but you could try mixing up to eight different patterns!

Jewellery Roll

Store and protect your necklaces, rings and bracelets in this delightful padded roll. It's perfect for travelling and what a lovely gift for the jewellery lover!

What you need:

Four pieces of fabric measuring 15 x 9in (38 x 23cm), one for the outside, one for the inside and two for the lining

A piece of $\frac{1}{8}$in (3mm) wadding/batting measuring the same

A piece of fabric measuring 9 x 2in (23 x 5cm) for the ring roll

A press stud

A handful of toy stuffing

50in (127cm) of 1in (2.5cm) bias binding

Two 8in (20.3cm) nylon zips

28in (71cm) of ribbon

Two 9in (23cm) strips of lace and one of ribbon, to decorate

Loop turner

1 Firstly, for the ring roll, sew the two long sides of the fabric right sides together.

2 Fold so that the seam sits in the centre, and sew across one end. Using a loop turner or something similar, turn the right way out.

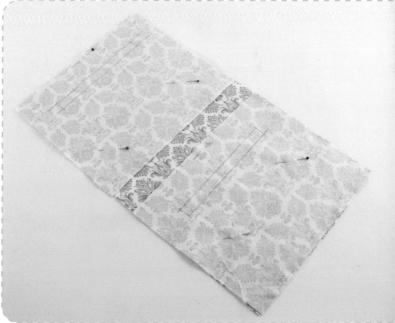

3 Fill with the toy stuffing, leaving a gap of about ½in (13mm) at the open end to give room to sew into the jewellery roll, then sew one side of the press stud to the closed end.

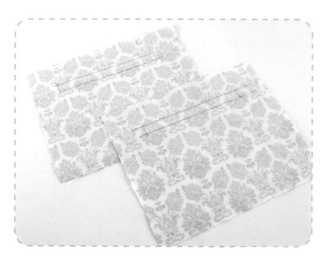

4 Take one piece of the lining fabric and cut in half widthways. Trim 1in (2.5cm) from the length of each piece.

5 Draw two boxes centrally, measuring ½ x 6in (13mm x 15cm). They should be 1½in (4cm) from the top edges of the lining fabric, as in the photograph. These will be the positions of the zips.

6 Lay these pieces right sides together with the inside fabric, as shown, leaving a gap in the centre, and pin.

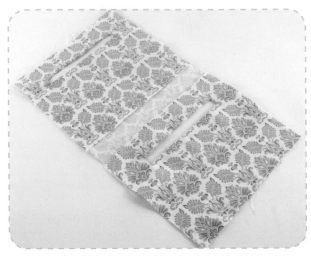

7 Sew along the drawn lines. Cut straight down the centre of each box with small scissors. When you come to the end, snip into the corners, avoiding cutting the stitches.

8 Turn the right way out and press. This may seem impossible but it really does work!

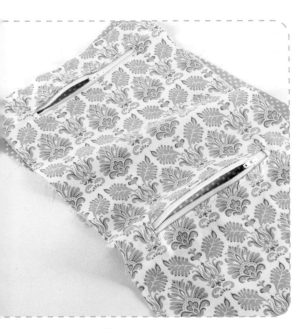

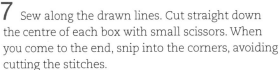

9 Place the zips behind these windows, tack/baste in place, then sew.

10 Lay this section, right side up, on top of the second piece of lining, and that in turn on top of the wadding/batting. Pin then sew all the way round, close to the raw edges.

11 Sew straight across the pouch, 5in (12.7cm) down from the top zip, and 1in (2.5cm) above the other zip, to make the pockets.

12 Lay the ring roll across the centre, and tack/baste the open end to the raw edge.

13 To decorate the front of the pouch, sew the strips of ribbon and lace across one end.

14 Place the pocket section on top, and pin together. Make sure the pretty side of your fabric is showing. Apply the bias binding all the way round (see page 15).

15 Sew the second part of the press stud in place so that the ring roll is secured to the edge of the pouch.

16 Finally, fold the ribbon in half and stitch the centre of it into one of the centre seams on the outside of your jewellery roll.

17 And roll!

Tip:
You could easily make two ring rolls if you need more storage.

Bunting

Bunting never seems to date, suits any room, uses very little fabric and is so easy to make! Drape it across the window, the bed-head, the furniture… anywhere that looks bare and in need of a bit of decoration.

1 Cut your fabric into triangles, measuring 4in (10cm) across the top and 8in (20.3cm) to the point.

2 Place two triangles right sides together and sew down the two sides, leaving the top open.

3 Snip across the point and turn the right way out. Press.

4 Using an over edge stitch (see page 13), hand sew the pennants to the cord, with even spaces in between.

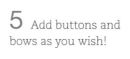

5 Add buttons and bows as you wish!

Tip

Little bells on the tips of the bunting make a delicate jingle in the breeze created by an open window.

Garment Protector

Keep your garments dust-free and beautifully presented. If you are giving a gift of clothing, this protector is the perfect finishing touch.

What you need:

A coat hanger

Patterned fabric measuring 20 x 7in (51 x 17.8cm)

Two strips of plain fabric to trim measuring 20 x 3in (51 x 7.5cm)

Lace measuring 39in (99cm)

Ribbon measuring 12in (30.5cm) and button for the bow

1 Fold the patterned fabric in half widthways, right sides together.

2 Place the coat hanger 2in (5cm) from the top (not including the hook). Draw an arc 1in (2.5cm) from the top of the hanger, using the hanger as your template. Extend the arc by 2in (5cm) on each side. Mark the position of the hook.

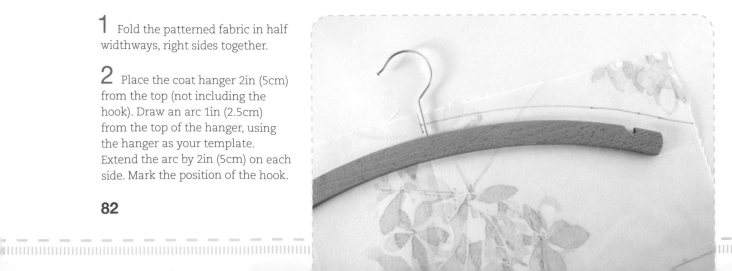

3 Cut out two pieces by cutting through both layers of the folded fabric.

4 Take the two strips of plain fabric, and sew right sides together across the bottom of the patterned fabric.

5 Sew both sides together, leaving a gap of about 1in (2.5cm) at the point you marked for the hook. Back tack (see page 14) either side of this gap to stop the stitches coming undone.

6 Fold the raw edge of the plain fabric over twice and top stitch to hem.

7 Turn right sides out and press. Take the strip of ribbon and pin then sew it all the way round the plain fabric trim. Add a little bow and button by hand to finish.

Tip
If you are a dressmaker, why not save a little of the same dress fabric to make the cover?

PICNIC TIME

This picnic suite really sets the scene for summer dining. On a balmy, sunny day, there is nothing more enjoyable than eating al fresco, with good food, good wine, good conversation and the smell of cut grass and freshly baked bread. The whole set of homemade picnic items would make a welcome gift for someone who loves the outdoor life, particularly if you fill the hamper with edible treats!

Picnic Place Mat

Keep your cutlery picnic-ready with this useful place mat and storage solution, and enjoy dining outdoors in style! You can roll the place mats up to store them, ready for their next outing.

What you need

For one mat:

Two rectangles of fabric measuring 14 x 10in (35.5 x 25.4cm)

One rectangle of 1/8 in (3mm) wadding/batting measuring the same

A strip of contrasting fabric measuring 14 x 5in (35.5 x 12.7cm)

One square of contrasting fabric for the pocket measuring 5 x 6in (12.7 x 15.3cm)

50in (127cm) bias binding; mine was edged in lace

6in (15.3cm) gingham ribbon

Repositionable adhesive spray

1 Take the contrasting strip of fabric, fold over the two long edges by ¼in (0.5cm), and press.

2 Place across the main fabric on the right side, two-thirds up from the bottom. Use the repositionable adhesive spray to keep it in place. Top stitch on your machine.

3 Fold over the top of the pocket by ¼in (0.5cm,) press and top stitch.

4 Fold inwards the remaining three sides by ¼in (0.5cm) and press.

5 Place the pocket over the contrasting strip on the right-hand side and sew the sides and base to make the pocket.

6 Spray the wrong side of the mat with repositionable adhesive spray and lay on top of the wadding/batting.

7 Spray again and lay this piece on top of the wrong side of the backing fabric. Round off the corners.

8 Stitch the bias binding around all four sides. Cover the join with a bow.

Tip
Roll the place mat for storage and tie with a matching ribbon.

Bread Bag

This cotton drawstring bag will keep your bread aerated so your crusts are crusty and your bread is fresher, so it is perfect for eating outdoors. If you bake as well as sew, it would also look great in the kitchen, filled with homemade bread!

What you need:

Piece of outer fabric measuring 24 x 10in (61 x 25.4cm)

Piece of lining fabric measuring the same

Two circles of fabric for the base and lining base, measuring 8in (20.3cm) across

23in (58.5cm) of 1in (2.5cm) bias binding or ribbon for the drawstring tape

50in (127cm) of string to tie

Safety pin

Air erasable pen

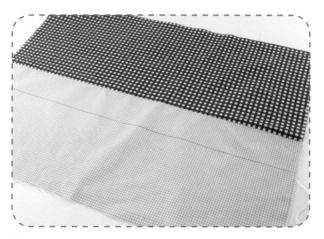

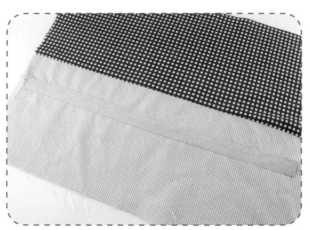

1 Sew the top of the outer bag to the top of the lining, right sides together.

2 Turn over to the right side, and with the air erasable pen, draw a line 3in (7.6cm) from the top of the outer side; this is your guide for where to attach the tape that will act as a channel for the drawstring.

3 Fold in the ends of the tape by about ½in (13mm) and sew along each edge, over the pen mark. Leave the ends open, and make sure the ends of the tape are just short of the fabric edges so they will not be sewn into the side seam of the bag.

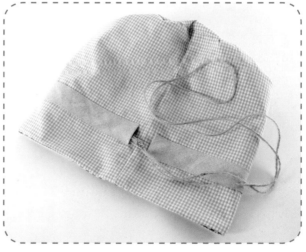

4 Sew together the side seam to make a tube. Pin one circle of base fabric to the end of the tube.

5 Sew round the circle. Repeat with the lining side, but leave a gap of about 3in (7.5cm) for turning.

6 Turn the right way out, and stitch the opening together with a ladder stitch (see page 13). Push the lining into the bag.

7 Fold the string in half and knot, then thread onto the safety pin and thread through the tape

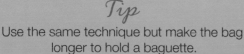

Tip
Use the same technique but make the bag longer to hold a baguette.

Jar Cover

Why shouldn't your jam and jelly jars be well dressed too? This is a simple little cap that can be made to fit any size of jar, and makes your homemade preserves look really special! It may seem a little extravagant to line the cover, but this is in fact much easier than trying to hem a circle.

What you need:

A jar

A circle of fabric measuring twice the size

A circle of lining fabric measuring the same

A piece of ¼in (0.5cm) elastic measuring around 10in (25.4cm); you will have some spare but it is easier to apply when it is longer than you need

A circle template, diameter 1in (2.5cm) larger than your lid

Air erasable pen

1 Place the two circles right sides together and sew all the way round, leaving a gap of around 2in (5cm) for turning.

2 Snip into the curve, then turn the right way out. Press, then sew closed the opening with a ladder stitch (see page 13).

3 Draw a circle on the lining side of the fabric with an air erasable pen, using your template which is slightly larger than the lid.

4 Pin the elastic over this line and back tack a couple of stitches to secure the end.

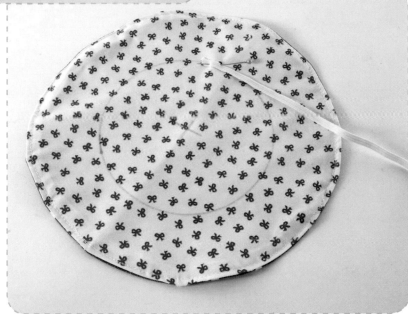

5 Using either a straight or zigzag stitch, slowly guide the elastic over your pen mark and sew, gently pulling the elastic so that the fabric gathers.

6 When the circle is complete, back tack again and snip away the excess elastic.

Tip
Find strawberry, orange or lemon prints according to what is contained in the jar.

Picnic Pillow

Half a yard of fabric will easily make one pillow cover, so you can enjoy your picnic in comfort! This envelope style involves no zips or hand sewing, so is simple for a beginner to make.

What you need:

One 14in (35.5cm) pillow pad

Fabric measuring 15in (38cm) square

Two pieces of fabric, each measuring 15 x 10in (38 x 25.3cm)

Contrasting fabric measuring 15 x 4in (38 x 10cm)

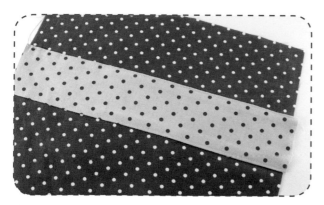

1 Take the rectangle of contrasting fabric and press the two long edges over by ½in (13mm).

2 Pin across the square of fabric, about a third of the way down, then top stitch the edges.

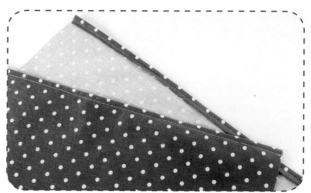

3 Take the two rectangles of fabric, and make a hem along one 15in (38cm) side of each by folding over twice and top stitching.

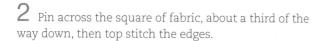

4 Lay the front of the pillow cover right side up, then place the first rectangle right side down on top of this, with the hemmed side in the middle. Pin.

5 Pin the second rectangle to the opposite side, again with the hemmed side to the centre. The two panels should overlap. Sew all the way round.

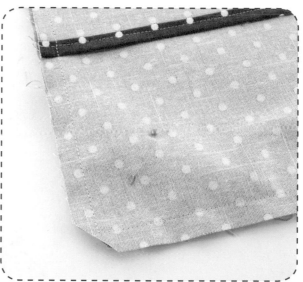

6 Snip across the corners. Turn the right way out and press.

Tip
If it suits your fabric, you could add a tassel to each corner.

Bottle Bag

This makes perfectly presented wine for the picnic table, or a stylish gift bag for a bottle of wine. The little pocket on the side is a handy place to keep the cork. Cheers!

What you need:

For the outside of the bag, fabric measuring 9 x 12in (22.8 x 30.5cm)

Contrasting fabric measuring 12 x 3½in (30.5 x 9cm)

For the lining, fabric measuring 12 x 2in (30.5 x 5cm)

For the pocket, fabric measuring 4in (10cm) square

11½in (29.2cm) of ¾in (19mm) bias binding or ribbon for the drawstring tape

24in (61cm) of string to tie

Safety pin

Air erasable pen

1 Sew the contrasting fabric right sides together to the top of the outer fabric.

2 Draw a line 1½in (3.8cm) from the top with air erasable pen. This is where you will sew the tape that will act as a channel for the drawstring.

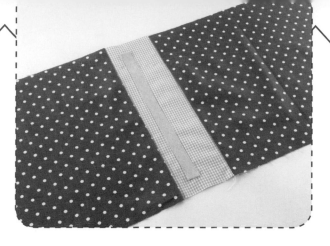

3 Folding in each end, top stitch the tape along your drawn line. Leave a gap of about 1in (2.5cm) at each end as you do not want the tape to get caught in the seam.

4 Sew the top of the outer layer to the top of the lining.

5 Take the pocket fabric, fold over the top and hem. Fold the other three edges over and press. Place onto the front of the outer fabric and sew round three sides, leaving the top open.

6 Fold the fabric into a long tube and sew all the way down the side, leaving a gap in the lining section for turning. Fold so that the seam is in the centre, then sew across the top and bottom.

7 Pull open the base of the bag, so that the seam is parallel to the side.

8 Draw a line across the seam, 1in (2.5cm) from the point. Do this on both sides. Sew across the line and cut off the excess fabric. Repeat at the other end of the bag.

9 Turn the bag the right way out and press. Push the lining inside the bag. Fold the string in half and knot. Thread the end onto a safety pin and thread through the tape.

Index